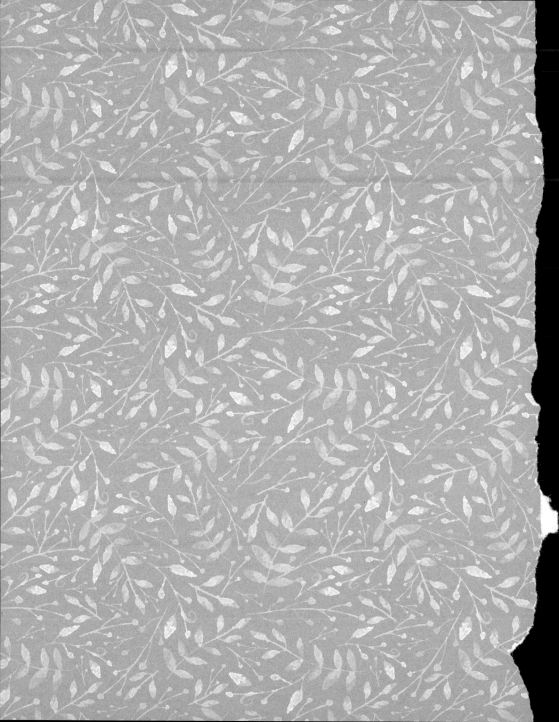

A SUMMER WITH
Great-Aunt Rose

A SUMMER WITH
Great-Aunt Rose

A PARABLE BY
DIETER F. UCHTDORF

WITH ILLUSTRATIONS BY
SALVADOR ALVAREZ

DESERET
BOOK

SALT LAKE CITY, UTAH

Adapted from a talk given at the general women's
session of general conference, October 2015.

Text © 2016 Dieter F. Uchtdorf
Illustrations © 2016 Salvador G. Alvarez

Library of Congress Cataloging-in-Publication Data

Names: Uchtdorf, Dieter F., author. | Alvarez, Salvador, 1951– illustrator.
Title: A summer with Great-Aunt Rose / a parable by Dieter F. Uchtdorf ; Illustrated
     by Salvador Alvarez.
Description: Salt Lake City, Utah : Deseret Book, [2016] | ?2016 | Includes biblio-
     graphical references.
Identifiers: LCCN 2016011266 | ISBN 9781629722528 (hardbound : alk. paper)
Subjects: LCSH: Happiness—Religious aspects—The Church of Jesus Christ of Latter-
     day Saints. | Christian life—Mormon authors. | Mormon women—Fiction. |
     LCGFT: Parables.
Classification: LCC BX8643.H35 U24 2016 | DDC 248.4/89332—dc23 LC record
     available at http://lccn.loc.gov/2016011266

Printed in China
RR Donnelley, Shenzhen, China

10   9   8   7   6   5   4   3   2   1

Eye hath not seen,

NOR EAR HEARD,

neither have entered into the heart of man,

the things which God hath prepared

for them that love him.

—1 CORINTHIANS 2:9

*O*ften, when I am preparing a message, my thoughts turn to the way the Savior taught. It is interesting how He was able to teach the most sublime truths using simple stories. His parables invited His disciples to embrace truths not just with their minds but also with their hearts and to connect eternal principles with their everyday lives.[1]

I too will share my message in these pages by expressing my thoughts and feelings in the form of a story. I invite you to read with the Spirit. The Holy Ghost will help you to find the message for you in this parable.

The story is about a girl named Eva. There are two important things you should know about Eva. One is that she was eleven years old in this story. And the other is that she absolutely, positively did not want to go and live with her great-aunt Rose.

Not at all.

NO WAY.

But Eva's mother was going to have surgery that required a lengthy recovery. So Eva's parents were sending her to spend the summer with Great-Aunt Rose.

In Eva's mind, there were a thousand reasons why this was a bad idea. For one thing, it would mean being away from her mother. It would also mean leaving her family and friends. And besides, she didn't even know Great-Aunt Rose. She was quite comfortable, thank you very much, right where she was.

But no amount of arguing or eye rolling could change the decision. So Eva packed up a suitcase and took the long drive with her father to Great-Aunt Rose's house.

*F*rom the moment Eva stepped inside the house, she hated it.

EVERYTHING WAS SO OLD!

Every inch of the place was packed with old books, strange-colored bottles, and plastic bins spilling over with beads, bows, and buttons.

Great-Aunt Rose lived there alone; she had never married. The only other inhabitant was a gray cat who liked to find the highest point in every room and perch there, staring like a hungry tiger at everything below.

Even the house itself seemed lonely. It was out in the countryside, where the houses are far apart. No one Eva's age lived within half a mile. That made Eva feel lonely too.

At first she didn't pay much attention to Great-Aunt Rose. She mostly thought about her mother. Sometimes, she would stay awake at night, praying with all her soul that her mother would be well. And though it didn't happen right away, Eva began to feel that

God was

watching
OVER HER MOTHER.

Word finally came that the operation was a success, and now all that was left for Eva to do was to endure till the end of summer. But oh, how she hated enduring!

With her mind now at ease about her mother, Eva began to notice Great-Aunt Rose a little more. She was a large woman—everything about her was large: her voice, her smile, her personality. It wasn't easy for her to get around, but she always sang and laughed while she worked, and the sound of her laughter filled the house. Every night she sat down on her overstuffed sofa, pulled out her scriptures, and read out loud. And as she read, she sometimes made comments like

"Oh, he shouldn't have done that!"

or

"What wouldn't I give to have been there!"

or

"ISN'T THAT THE MOST BEAUTIFUL THING YOU'VE EVER HEARD!"

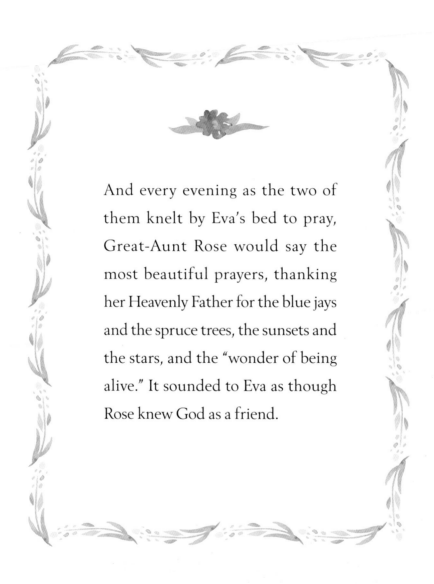

And every evening as the two of
them knelt by Eva's bed to pray,
Great-Aunt Rose would say the
most beautiful prayers, thanking
her Heavenly Father for the blue jays
and the spruce trees, the sunsets and
the stars, and the "wonder of being
alive." It sounded to Eva as though
Rose knew God as a friend.

*O*ver time, Eva made a surprising discovery: Great-Aunt Rose was quite possibly the happiest person she had ever known!

But how could that be?

WHAT DID SHE HAVE TO BE HAPPY ABOUT?

She had never married, she had no children, she had no one to keep her company except that creepy cat, and she had a hard time doing simple things like tying her shoes and walking up stairs.

When she went to town, she wore embarrassingly big, bright hats. But people didn't laugh at her. Instead, they crowded around her, wanting to talk to her. Rose had been a schoolteacher, and it wasn't uncommon for former students—now grown up with children of their own—to stop and chat. They thanked her for being a good influence in their lives. They often laughed. Sometimes they even cried.

As the summer progressed, Eva spent more and more time with Rose. They went on long walks, and Eva learned the difference between sparrows and finches. She picked wild elderberries and made marmalade from oranges. She learned about her great-great-grandmother who left her beloved homeland, sailed across an ocean, and walked across the plains to be with the Saints.

Soon Eva made another startling discovery: not only was Great-Aunt Rose *one of the happiest persons she knew,* but Eva herself was HAPPIER whenever she was around her.

The days of summer were passing more quickly now. **BEFORE EVA KNEW IT,** Great-Aunt Rose said it would soon be time for Eva to return

HOME.

Though Eva had been looking forward to that moment since the day she had arrived, she wasn't quite sure how to feel about it now. She realized **SHE WAS ACTUALLY GOING TO MISS** this strange old house with the stalker cat and her *beloved* GREAT-AUNT *Rose.*

The day before her father arrived to pick her up, Eva asked the question she had been wondering about for weeks: "Aunt Rose, why are you so happy?"

Great-Aunt Rose looked at her carefully and then guided her to a painting that hung in the front room. It had been a gift from a talented dear friend.

"WHAT DO YOU SEE THERE?"

she asked.

*E*va had noticed the painting before, but she hadn't really looked at it closely. A girl in pioneer dress skipped along a bright blue path. The grass and trees were a vibrant green. Eva said, "It's a painting of a girl. Looks like she's skipping."

"Yes, it is a pioneer girl skipping along happily," Great-Aunt Rose said. "I imagine there were many dark and dreary days for the pioneers. Their life was so hard—we can't even imagine. But in this painting, everything is BRIGHT AND HOPEFUL. This girl has a spring in her step, and she is moving forward and upward."

Eva was silent, so Great-Aunt Rose continued: "There is enough that doesn't go right in life to make just about anyone liable to get worked into a puddle of pessimism and a mess of melancholy. But I know people who, even when things don't work out, *focus on the wonders and miracles of life.* Those folks are the happiest people I know."

"But," Eva said, "you can't just flip a switch and go from sad to happy."

No, perhaps not," Great-Aunt Rose smiled gently, "but God didn't design us to be sad.

HE CREATED US
to have joy!

So if we trust Him, He will help us to notice the good, bright, hopeful things of life. And sure enough, the world will become brighter. No, it doesn't happen instantly, but honestly, how many good things do?

Seems to me that *the best things,*

 like homemade bread or orange marmalade,

TAKE PATIENCE AND WORK."

Eva thought about it a moment and said, "Maybe it's not so simple for people who don't have everything perfect in their lives."

21

*D*ear Eva, do you really think that my life is perfect?" Great-Aunt Rose sat with Eva on the overstuffed sofa. "There was a time when I was so discouraged I didn't want to go on."

"You?" Eva asked.

Great-Aunt Rose nodded. "There were so many things I wished for in my life." As she spoke, a sadness entered her voice that Eva had never heard before. "Most of them never happened. It was one heartbreak after another. One day I realized that things would never be the way I had hoped for. That was a depressing day.

I WAS READY TO GIVE UP
AND BE MISERABLE."

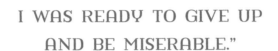

"So what did you do?"

"Nothing for a time. I was just angry. I was an absolute monster to be around." Then she laughed a little, but it was not her usual big, room-filling laugh. "'It's not fair' was the song I sang over and over in my head. But eventually

I DISCOVERED SOMETHING
THAT TURNED MY WHOLE
LIFE AROUND."

"What was it?"

"FAITH"

Great-Aunt Rose smiled. "I discovered faith. And faith led to hope. And faith and hope gave me confidence that one day everything would make sense, that because of the Savior, all the wrongs would be made right. After that, I saw that the path before me wasn't as dreary and dusty as I had thought. I began to notice the bright blues, the verdant greens, and the fiery reds. And I decided I had a choice—

I could hang my head and drag my feet on the dusty road of self-pity,

or

I COULD HAVE A LITTLE FAITH, PUT ON A BRIGHT DRESS, SLIP ON MY DANCING SHOES, AND SKIP DOWN THE PATH OF LIFE, SINGING AS I WENT."

 Now her voice was skipping along like the girl in the painting.

Great-Aunt Rose reached over to the end table and pulled her well-worn scriptures onto her lap. "I don't think I was clinically depressed—I'm not sure you can talk yourself out of that. But I sure had talked myself into being miserable! Yes, I had some dark days, but all my brooding and worrying wasn't going to change that—it was only making things worse. Faith in the Savior taught me that no matter what had happened in the past, my story could have a happy ending."

How do you know that?" Eva asked.

Great-Aunt Rose turned a page in her Bible and said, "It says it right here:"

God

. . . will dwell with them,

and they shall be his people, and God himself

shall be with them, and be their God.

AND GOD SHALL WIPE AWAY

ALL TEARS FROM THEIR EYES;

and there shall be no more death, neither sorrow,

nor crying, neither shall there be any more pain:

for the former things are passed away.[3]

Rose looked at Eva. Her smile was wide as she whispered, with a slight quiver in her voice, "Isn't that the most beautiful thing you've ever heard?"

It really did sound beautiful, Eva thought.

Great-Aunt Rose turned a few pages and pointed to a verse for Eva to read:

Eye hath not seen, NOR EAR HEARD, neither have entered into the heart of man, *the things which God hath prepared for them that love him.*[4]

With such a glorious future," Great-Aunt Rose said, "why get swallowed up in past or present things that don't go quite the way we planned?"

Eva furrowed her brow. "But wait a minute," she said. "Are you saying that being happy means just looking forward to happiness in the future? Is all our happiness in eternity? Can't some of it happen now?"

"Oh, of course it can!" Rose exclaimed. "Dear child, now is part of eternity. It doesn't only begin after we die!

FAITH AND HOPE WILL OPEN YOUR EYES TO THE HAPPINESS THAT IS PLACED BEFORE YOU.

"I know a poem that says,

Forever

—IS COMPOSED OF NOWS.[5]

I didn't want my forever to be composed of dark and fearful 'Nows.' And I didn't want to live in the gloom of a bunker, gritting my teeth, closing my eyes, and resentfully enduring to the bitter end. Faith gave me the hope I needed to live joyfully now!"

"So what did you do then?" Eva asked.

"I exercised faith in God's promises by filling my life with meaningful things. I went to school. I got an education. That led me to a career that I loved."

*E*va thought about that for a moment and finally said, "But surely being busy isn't what made you happy. There are a lot of busy people who aren't happy."

"How can you be so wise for someone so young?" Great-Aunt Rose asked. "You're absolutely right. And most of those busy, unhappy people have forgotten the one thing that matters most in all the world—the thing Jesus said is the heart of His gospel."

"And what is that?" Eva asked.

"*It is* LOVE –
THE PURE LOVE OF CHRIST,"

Rose said. "You see, everything else in the gospel—all the shoulds and the musts and the thou shalts—lead to love. When we LOVE GOD, we want to SERVE HIM. We want to BE LIKE HIM. When we love our neighbors, we stop thinking so much about our own problems and help others to solve theirs."[6]

"And that is what makes us happy?" Eva asked.

Great-Aunt Rose nodded and smiled, her eyes filling with tears.

"YES, MY DEAR.
That is what makes us
HAPPY."

The next day Eva hugged her great-aunt Rose and thanked her for everything she had done. She returned home to her family and her friends and her house and her neighborhood.

But she was never quite the same.

As Eva grew older, she often thought
of the words of her great-aunt Rose.
Eva eventually married, raised children,

AND LIVED A *long* AND
wonderful LIFE.

*A*nd one day, as she was standing in her own home, admiring a painting of a girl in pioneer dress skipping down a bright blue path, she realized that somehow she had reached the same age her great-aunt Rose was during that remarkable summer.

When she realized this, she felt a special prayer swell within her heart. And Eva felt GRATEFUL for her life, for her family, for the restored gospel of Jesus Christ, and for that summer so long ago when Great-Aunt Rose[7] taught her about

FAITH, HOPE, AND LOVE.[8]

My dear friend in Christ, I hope and pray that something in this story has touched your heart and inspired your soul.

I KNOW THAT *God lives* AND THAT HE LOVES YOU.

As you walk along your own bright path of discipleship, I pray that faith will fortify every footstep along your way; that hope will open your eyes to the glories Heavenly Father has in store for you; and that love for God and all His children will fill your heart.

1. See, for example, Matthew 13:24–30; 18:23–35; 20:1–16; 22:1–14; 25; Luke 10:25–37; 15:11–32.

2. See 2 Nephi 2:25.

3. Revelation 21:3–4.

4. 1 Corinthians 2:9.

5. "Forever—is composed of Nows," in *Final Harvest: Emily Dickinson's Poems,* sel. Thomas H. Johnson (1961), 158; see also poetryfoundation.org/poem/182912.

6. See Luke 9:24.

7. "Often the prickly thorn produces tender roses" (Ovid, *Epistulae ex ponto,* book 2, epistle 2, line 34; "Saepe creat molles aspera spina rosas").

8. See Moroni 7:42–48.

President Dieter F. Uchtdorf has served as the Second Counselor in the First Presidency of The Church of Jesus Christ of Latter-day Saints since February 3, 2008. He was sustained as a member of the Quorum of the Twelve Apostles in October 2004. He became a General Authority in April 1994 and served as a member of the Presidency of the Seventy from August 2002 until his call to the Twelve.

Prior to his calling as a General Authority, President Uchtdorf was the senior vice president of flight operations and chief pilot of Lufthansa German Airlines.

President Uchtdorf was born in 1940 in what is now the Czech Republic. He grew up in Zwickau, Germany, where his family joined the Church in 1947. He and his wife, Harriet Reich Uchtdorf, are the parents of two children and have six grandchildren and one great-granddaughter.

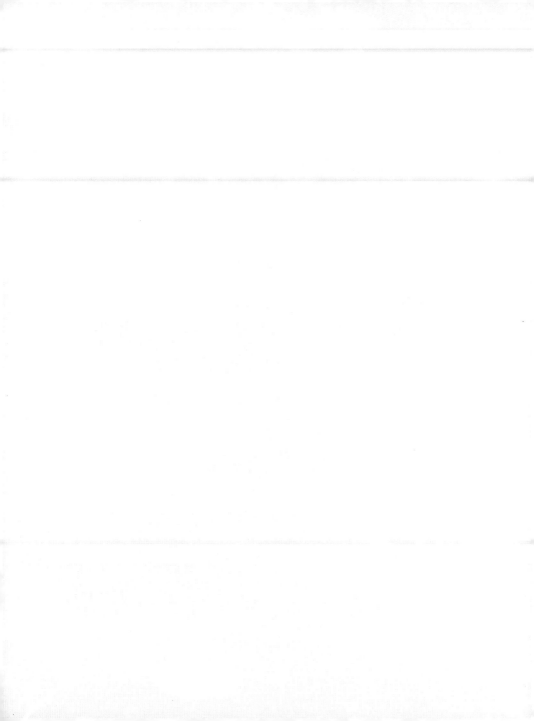

Salvador Alvarez has been an artist his whole life. As a young man he studied under Sebastian Capella in oil painting and drawing, and Stanahous Sowinski in watercolor. Later he was awarded a full scholarship to the master's program at the New York Academy of Art. He is currently working on the "Joy in the Journey" pioneer collection.

Visit the artist and view more of his paintings at www.SalvadorAlvarez.com.

DESIGN CREDITS

Book design © 2016 Deseret Book Company
Art direction by Richard Erickson
Design by Sheryl Dickert Smith

Cover old paper frame under illustration, Shutterstock © Alexandr Makarov.

Cover background floral texture, Shutterstock © eugenia bacon.

Cover background color and cream background used for interior, Shutterstock © Alisa Burkovska.

Endsheets background pattern, Shutterstock © Tatiana_Kost.

Interior leaf frames and embellishments/floral embellishments, page 29; daisy in center of embellishment, page 15; paint line to make frame, pages 1, 17, 36, and cover; elements for leaf border for cover, pages 17, 22, 23, 28, 29; and embellishments pages 24 and 31, Shutterstock © Tatiana_Kost.

Interior floral embellishments pages i, iii, 1, 2, 9, 10, 15, 16, 21, 22, 33, 36; elements to make wreath page v; frame page 9, Shutterstock © Olga Lebedeva.

Interior wreath page 33, Shutterstock © zorina_larisa.

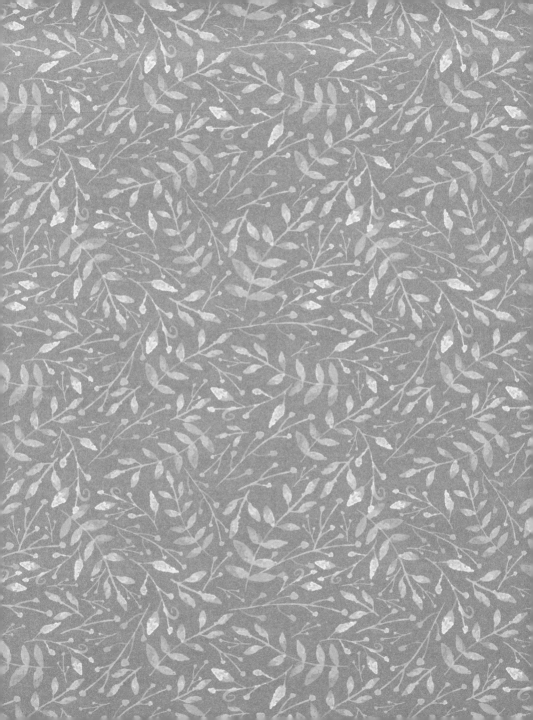

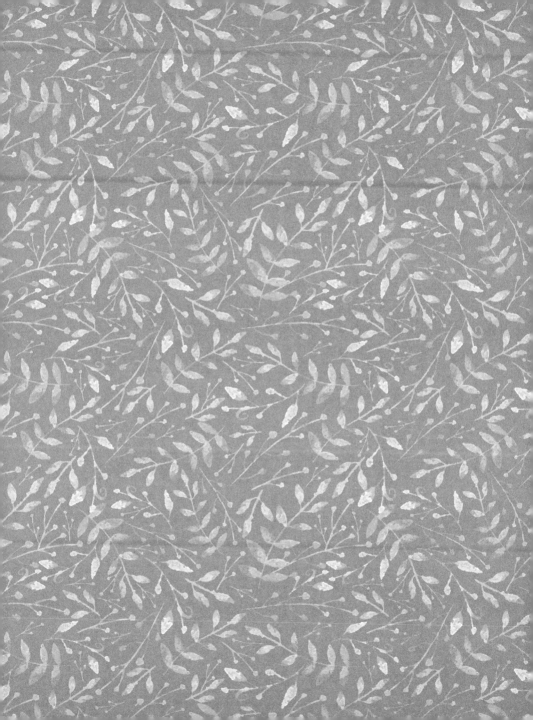